Escape ~~from Indian~~

Captivity

THE STORY
of
MARY DRAPER INGLES
and son
THOMAS INGLES

as told by
JOHN INGLES, SR.

Edited by
ROBERTA INGLES STEELE
and
ANDREW LEWIS INGLES

First Edition 1969

Second Edition 1982

Sixth Printing

Copyright 1969 by Roberta Ingles Steele
and Andrew Lewis Ingles
Box 3485, FSS, Radford, Virginia 24143

Library of Congress Catalog Card Number: 82-61258
ISBN 0-318-03613-4

FOREWORD

The Mary Draper Ingles story has been told and re-told many times, sometimes with not enough regard for historical facts.

Our great great grandfather, John Ingles, Sr., wrote an account of these frontier days experiences as told to him repeatedly by his father, William Ingles, and mother, Mary Draper Ingles. His manuscript is preserved in the University of Virginia Library.

John Ingles, Sr., was *born June 18, 1766, some ten years after his mother's return from captivity. Since Mary Draper Ingles died in 1815, her son, John, had ample years to discuss these events with his mother from the viewpoint of a mature adult as well as learning these accounts as a child.

We have tried to decipher the original manuscript accurately — preserving the written style of the author as to spelling, choice of words, punctuation, and use of capitals. Certain footnotes have been added to support dates and facts, and in some cases to explain or add relative and new information to assist in understanding the narrative.

PROOF OF AUTHORSHIP

Master Graphoanalyst, Mrs. Myrtle McCleary Lednum, of Norfolk, Virginia, compared the signatures and other forms of the will and manuscript of John Ingles, Senior and made the following statement: "Having applied the principles of Graphoanalysis to the study of both manuscript and will it is my opinion that the manuscript signed by John Ingles Sn. and the will signed by John Ingles Senr. (codicil signed John Ingles Sn.) were written by one and the same person."** This statement greatly encouraged us to publish this manuscript.

---

*Death date was July 16, 1836.
**The abbreviations of the word, senior, appear in Mrs. Lednum's statement as written by John Ingles in his documents mentioned above.

EDITOR'S NOTE

William Ingles was born in London, England, 1729, and his wife, Mary Draper, was born in Philadelphia, Pennsylvania, in 1732. They were married at Draper's Meadow in 1750 and were the parents of six children. Thomas and George were born at Draper's Meadow and captured by the Indians, July 30, 1755. Thirteen years later Thomas was rescued by his father, but George, the younger son, died in captivity. Mary, Susan, Rhoda, and John were born at Ingles Ferry.

Thomas Ingles married Ellinor Grills of Albemarle County, Virginia. Mary married John Grills; Susan married Abraham Trigg; Rhoda married Byrd Smith; and John married Margaret Crockett.

John Ingles was born June 18, 1766, and married Margaret Crockett April 22, 1794. They had nine children: William, Mary, Samuel, Crockett, Malinda, Lockey, John, Margaret, and Thomas. John's first wife, Margaret, died October 26, 1810. January 27, 1814, John married Elizabeth Saunders—who lived until August 4, 1834. John died two years later—July 16, 1836 and was buried at Ingles Ferry.

When he was only fifty-three years old, William Ingles died and was buried at Ingles Ferry in 1782. His wife, Mary Draper Ingles, remained at the homeplace until her death in 1815.

INTRODUCTION

At the repeated solicitations of my relations and friends of which letters in my possession are suffitiant evidance, I have consented to write the following short history The application has been made to me as I am the only branch of my Fathers familey now in existance, who knows of the defficulties and sufferings my fathers own familey had to undergo at that early day, in attempting to settle this Western World. Though the greater part of the transactions to which allusion is made happened long before I was born yet having heard them so frequantly repeated by my father and mother in my early days they made such deep and lasting impressions on my youthfull mind that they will never be forgotten by me as long is I live and I believe are as fresh in my memory at this day as they ever was, I will therefore endevour to give a short but correct narative of the scens through which they had to pass in their first settling on the Western Watters of Virginia so fare as my recollection serves me at this time that a record of them may be preserved for the gratification of our friends and rising generation, However fabulous or romantick the narative may appear in some of its parts to many persons they are stubborn facts that could have been abundantly established by many witnesses at an earley day it been reqired.

John Ingles Sn

ACKNOWLEDGMENTS

In 1934 Dr. Virginia O'Rear Hudson, Professor of English at Radford College (now Radford University) assisted our father, William Ingles (1877-1966), in transcribing this manuscript. Her efforts in this respect have been most useful to the editors. We also wish to acknowledge our indebtedness to: Edmund Berkeley, Jr., Curator of Manuscripts at the University of Virginia; Alfred K. Guthe, Editor of the **Tennessee Archaeologist**; Mrs. Mildred R. Shirk, past Regional Director of Montgomery-Radford Regional Library; Rev. Harold J. Dudley, Editor of the Third Edition of **Trans-Allegheny Pioneers** by John P. Hale; Dr. Elmer D. Johnson, Professor of History at Radford University; Cecil C. Lawson, certified land surveyor; and Mrs. Myrtle McCleary Lednum, Master Graphoanalyst, for their cooperation, research, and advice.

We also wish to express appreciation to Frances McCalla Ingles, Paul Warren Steele, Robert Perry Steele, and Anne Ingles for their interest, suggestions, and encouragement.

THE STORY OF MARY DRAPER INGLES

My Father William Ingles moved to the Western part of Virginia sometime about the year 1750 with my Grandfather his father in law George Draper and his familey and settled nearley on the top of the Alleganey mountains at a place then called Drapers Meadows now called Smithfield and at this time owned by Col. James Preston[1] at that time there was but few familey if any besides their own on the west side of the alleganey in this section of country However other famileys shortly after emigrated to it and made scattering settlements at some distance from each other and continued to Injoy peace and harmoney among them for 3 or 4 years in the meantime there had been severale parteys of the northern Indians, to wit, the Shawneys passed by where my Grandfather lived on their way to the South and wood Commit depredations on the Cawtauba Indians but was still friendley to the Whites at that time however this hapey state of things did not last long the Indians found out that they (M.S. faulty) gratify their Hethan thirst for bloodshead and plunder much nearer Home and at length commenced a warfair on the fronteer settlements & at a time it was little expected a partey of Shawneys fell in upon my fathers familey and an uncles familey John Draper which lived at the same place and killed severale and took the balance prisoners, to wit, my

[1]"Thomas, John and William Ingles, of Ingles' Mill Creek of the North Fork of Roanoke, were among the most interesting of the early settlers . . . William Ingles came to the Roanoke with his father and Uncle John before 1746. The land on which they lived seems to have belonged to William. He appears first as a worker on the road and later as a constable and militia officer. In May, 1750, he reported that the county funds collected by him had been consumed by the fire when his house burned. The date of his marriage to Mary Draper. is given as 1750, but he continued to live on the Roanoke until after 1753, when he purchased land at Draper's Meadows from Col. Patton. He was on the waters of New River in 1754 and 1755." F. B. Kegley, **Kegley's Virginia Frontier** (The Stone Press. 1938), pp. 194-195.

mother and her 2 children Thos. 4 yrs & George 2 & Aunt Draper & others[2] My grandmother Draper being a widow at that time & livin with my father was killed by (M.S. faulty) Col. Patton who was there who had a large claim of land in (Blot on M.S.) waters was killed, also, & some other persons not recolected My mother and her two children, Thos. the older 4 years old, and George abot 2 years old was taken as prisoners also my Aunt Draper who was wounded in her arm and Broke by a Ball which was shot at her in attempting to escape & severale others it so happened they made the attack on their harvest day and although there were severale men at the place the Indians took the advantage of attacking the Hows while the men (M.S. faulty) at their work in the harvest field and the field being some distance (M.S. faulty) the howse new nothing of the attack untill it was Intierly out of Their power to render any survice to the familey My father when Hearing the allarm run up verry near to the howse thinking perhaps he might render some survice in some way although entierly unarmed the Indians discovering him two stout active Indians took after him with their tome-hocks expecting to outrun him and kill him with their tome-hocks & was very near affecting their purpose & nothing but a providential act saved him while the Indians were persuing him & gaining on him very fast one on each sid at some distance running through the woods where it was a little thick with brush & undergrowth, fortunately in jumping over a logg fell The Indians being so eager in persuit over run him my father on rising amediately Tacked

[2]" . . . the Draper's Meadow massacre in which Col Patton was killed came on July 30. In this massacre there were killed, besides Col. Patton, Casper Barger and Mrs. Draper and child. James Cull was wounded and Mrs. Ingles and two children, Mrs. Draper, Jr., and Henry Leonard were taken prisoners. Preston's Register." F. B. Kegley's **Kegley's Virginia Frontier** (The Stone Press, 1938), p. 210.

back the other way and by that means made his escape as
there was no chance for what white men that was there
to render any releaf to the prisoners The Indians securing
all the guns they had which was in the howse & so few
settlers in the Country and them so fare distant apart that
They had to abandon all Idea of aney farther persuit after them. The Indians went off entierly unmolested they
gathered up their prisoners & plunder and started & steared
their cource down the New River They made but slow
progress in getting on as their way was much Impeded by
the thickness of the forrest & undergroath which covered
the whole country However on striking New River they
persued on down it. The Indians having several Horses
along packed with their plunder which they Had taken &
the prisoners mett with considerable Defiqualty in getting
on & the prisoners very roughly treated However from
some cause (M.S. faulty) my mother said that they always
treated her with more respect (M.S. faulty) aney of the
other prisoners and permitted her to ride on one of the
horses the greater part of the rod and to carry her children
though my Aunt Draper who had her arm broke was prin-
cipally put under her cear and my mother had to dress her
wound and to procure stuff to dress it and wood frequantly
send her off by herself into the woods to Hunt the wild com-
phisey to put to the broken arm and would be gone a considerable time and said she might had frequant oppertun-
iteys of leaving them but could not think of leaving her
children still Harbouring a hope that they might be persued or they might be all released togeather in some way
or Other They still worked on in this way untill they got
down some little Distance above the mouth of the great
Kanawa They came to a little salt spring in the Bank of
the river the Indians stoped there and rested for a day or

9

two there & with what kittles they Had with them boiled & mad some salt They then started on from there & persued this journey until they got to the nation where the Indians lived which was at the mouth of the Bigg Sioto & which took them about one month to performe from the time they were taken untill they arived at the nation. The next day after they got to the nation the prisoners had to undergo the Indian custom of running the gauntlett which was purformed by forming a two lines of all the Indians in the nation men women and children and the prisoners to start at the Head of the two rows formed & run down between the lines & every Indian giving them a cut or a pelt with switch sticks or such things as they could provide which was a very severe opperation and espitialy on my Aunt Draper whose arme had not got near well from the wound she had received when she was taken prisoner However my mother said she was exempted from that punishment and although she was treated with considerable (?) more than the other prisoners met with all the comfort left her was the hope that she might keep her two children with Her and to render (M.S. faulty) such survice as occation might need However a few days Baffiled all Her hopes The Indians partey collected in a few days after (?) who took prisoners and made a division of all the prisoners and her children taken away from her and consigned to different owners & was not permitted to asosiate to geather a tall Though trying as this circumstance was to her she was obliged to bear it and wore on under her applications in the best way she coud It so happened that there was some french traders there from detroit with some good trading with the Indians and as linen or Check shirts was great articles among the Indians and as my mother was a very good sewer she undertook to make some shirts for the traders at times when she was not Imployed Otherweys and as shirts was a scarce article among the Indians & one very much prised among them as a dress her permance pleased them so that they wood do any thing for her to get a shirt made and the frenchmen finding it a considerable advantage to them in selling their check & linnen to the Indians incouraged her very much & when she made a shirt for one of the Indians they would stick it upon a stick and run all through the town to show it & praise my mother what a fine squaw she was Then the frenchmen would make the Indians go to their store and pay her in goods to at least twice the value of the shirt She continued on in making shirts for them in this way while she stayed in this town which was two or three weeks & was making money very fast at about that time a party of the Indians started to the Bigg Bone lick which is now in the state of Kentuckey and took my mother & severale other of the prisoners to make salt[3] my mother being so distressed in being seperated from her children & her situation such a disagreeable one that she came to the determined resolution that she wood leave them & try to get Home or dy in the woods & prevailed on an old duch woman that was there and a prisoner too to engage with her in the seemingly Hopeless & daring attempt and as my mother was determined to make the attempt they arranged their plan which was to get leave of the Indians to go a peace from the Lick with a view to Hunt & geather some grapes & provided

[3]"In 1735, the Canadians who came to make war upon the Tchicachas (Chicksaws) found near the **fire river** or Ohio, the skeletons of seven elephants. x x x The place was near the **Ohio**, which in our maps of **Louisiana,** is marked with acrop."—Bossu's Travels (Lond. 1771—written "at the Illinois," 1756), Vol. I, pp. 179, 180. For other visits to these bones prior to the captivity of Mrs. Ingles, see, (1) Peale's **Account of the Mammoth** (London, 1802), pp. 8-10; Warren's **Mastodon Giganteus,** p. 1. (2) Gists **Journal in Pownall**, p.14." **Draper Manuscripts.** Series D. Vol. I. Chapter 6, p. 7 (The State Historical Society of Wisconsin).

themselves with a blankett and tomehock a peace & perhaps a knife and for fear of being Suspected took no other kind of clothing onley what was on them & those a good deal worn & started & as the Bigg Bone lick was 90 or 100 miles farther off than the camp and some little distance from the Ohio River they started in the after part of the day & steered their cource to strike the Ohio River which was all the guide they had to direct them I have frequantly Heard my mother say when she left the lick that she exchanged her tomehock with one of three frenchmen who was all sitting on One of the large Bones that was there and cracking walnuts at night the two women not returning the Indians became very uneasy thinking they had got a little of from the camp & were lost & used every exertions to find them not mistrusting their act and when they coud not find them concluded they had perished in the woods or (M.S. faulty) killed by some wild beast. This last circumstance was related to my father by some of the Indians who attended the treatey at point pleasant after the battle at the point and was the first time the Indians had heard what had become of my mother & old Duch woman. However on their getting to the river persued on up it & in the cource of 4 or 5 days reache the Indian town or rather on the opposite side of the Ohio river where there was a little corn raised & a cabbin They lay in the Cabbin all night and there was in the Cabbin some corn They ate of it and in the morning when they ware about starting ther Happened to be a (?) beast in the lot adjoining the cabbin They concluded to take it and pack on it what corn they coud to help them a long They did so and then started on a gain with the beast & corn and stearing on up the river & in sight of the Indian town & what was very extraordinary they saw severale Indian hunters that day &

12

They so secreeted themselves that they never discovered them There was a little river emptid into the Ohio (to wit) Lyching river on the side they ware and was two deap for them to wade all their chance was to travell up it untill they could find a passage and after traveleing up Liching 2 or 3 days found a place where the freshes had Drifted up timber across that afforded themselves a passage but How to get their beast over was at a loss at length the old duch woman insisted she coud take it over on the drift pile & made the attempt but after getting it on a peace the beast fell in among the logg & there they had to leave it They then took what corn they coud carry themselves & then moved down untill they struck the Ohio again & then pursued on up the Ohio and thus was the Cource they had to persuee at every stream of water that came in Their way of aney size & which there was severale & they could never have surmounted that defiqualty Had it not been at a season of the year when the water cources was very low & more so than common at the season eaven in this case was obliged to travele severale days Journey up severale of them before they could wade them & then down again to the Ohio which was their onley guide. They free-quantly in passing up & down those streams to find a pas-sage when they found the river made a bend & point of ridges (M.S. faulty) in wood attempt to cross these points of riges to shorten their distance and by being woorn down by fateigue & starvation wood have to pule them-selves up by the srubs & bushes till they got to the top and to decend they wood slide all the way down Under These defiqualteys and nothing to sustain nature but what they picked up in the woods such as black walnuts grapes pap-paws etc. & very often so pushed with hunger that they wood dig up roots & eate that they knew nothing of and

13

this extrematy the old duch woman getting disheart-
& discouraged got very ill natured to my mother &
ae some attempts to kill her blaiming my mother for
perswaiding her away & that they wood dye in the woods
and as she was a good deal stouter & stronger than my
mother she used every means to try to please the old
woman & keep her in a good Humer and at length get to
the mouth of the great Kanawa & then had performed but
very little more than one half of their Journey However
They persevered on up the Kanawa in the same manner
as they did the Ohio untill they got within 40 or 50 miles
of where my mother was taken prisoner (from) & the old
woman became more illnatured and made another attempt
to kill my mother & she thinks wood have affected it Had
she not by accident got loos from the old woman & being
somewhat more active & out run her this happened in the
evening Just before dusk my mother in making her escape
slipped under the river Bank & hid herself untile after Dark
and hearing nothing more of the old woman she crawled
out & in looking about the moon giving little light espied
a Cannoe at the bank of the river which was the same the
indians had taken them across on their way down on examining the Cannoe found it pritey much filled up with
leaves & Dirt which had blown into it but could not find a
pole or paddle in it She crawled up on the Bank luckeley
came a cross a thin slab which came off of a tree which
had been Blown down & shattered by the wind She took
the slab and went to the Cannoe & Cleaned out the leaves
& dirt Then pushed off the cannoe from the Bank and
got in it and although she never had any Knowledge of
stearing or workin a Cannoe before after making severale
tryals found she could stear her on & finiley crossed the
river to the other side it being at a place where some Hunt-

14

ers had made a little Improvement & built a cabbin the spring before & had planted some corn but the Buffalows & wild beasts had destroyed all the corn However my mother got into the cabbin and slept in the morning when she got out in the morning was examining about the little corn pack to find some corn or some thing she could eat discovered a little turnip or two which had escaped the wild beasts She pulled them and ate and at that time the old woman who was on the opposit side of the river saw my mother and Hallowed to her and begged very hard of my mother to come over to her again That she wood not do her aney harme However loth as my mother was to leave her after reflecting on how the old woman had treated her she thought perhaps the old woman might kill her and concluded that as she was out of her reach she had best keep so and from the hunters who hade made the settlement where she was before she was taken had geathered some eiday of the Distance she still had to perform and that the balance of the way she wood have to travele was a very rough one and although the little clothing which she had started with was nearley or entierly worn out or dragged off of her by the Brush on her long Journey & her mocosans intierly worn out that she had become litteralery naked and the weather growing cooler that her prospect of succeeding was almost a Hopeless one However, her resolution bore her up & she pursued on and to add to her defiqualtey There fell a little snow and all the Chance she had for keeping herself from perishing at night was to hunt out in the eavening a hollow logg or tree and geather leaves & put in it and then crawl in amongst the leaves & lye & after pursuing on in this manner for 4 or 5 days after leaving the old woman travelling through the frost and wading waters & round clifts of rocks that made in close

to the river She Became so frosted & her limbs so swelled
that it wood have been imposible she could have got aney
farther but that kind providence which had sustained her
through a Journey estimated not less than from 7 to 900
miles the rout which she was nessesarily obliged to travele
exposed to the Inclemancy of the weather & verosity of
wild beasts Hunger & starvation for forty two days and
a half in an unknown willderness still profided for her releaf it so happened that a man of the name of Adam Harmon and two of his Sones was at a place on New River
where they had settled and raised some corn that sumer
securing their corn and Hunting. When my mother got
to the improvement not seeing aney Howse began to
Hollow Harmon on hearing the voyce of a woman was a
good deal alarmed on listening being an old neighbour of
my mother and well acquainted with her voyce said to his
sons it certainly was Mary Ingles voice & knowing that
she was taken prisoner by the Indians was cautious there
might be Indians with her him and his sons Caught up
their guns and run on to where my mother was & you
may expect it was a Joyfull meating especialey to my
mother⁴ However they got her on to their Cabbin entierly
exosted & worn out by her expocers & starvation Harmon
Having plentey of fresh venison & Bear meat began to have
some cooked for her and having a pritey good knowledge
of her situation wood not suffer her to eate more than a
few mouthfulls at a time & by change her vituals in dif-

⁴"Adam Harman was born in Germany about the year 1724. He was
the oldest son of Heinrich Adam, and was about twenty years old when he
came, with his father, to New River. He and his next younger brother,
Henry (later known as Henry, Sr.), were perhaps the two sons, who with
their father in 1755, rescued Mrs. Mary Ingles, whom they found in their
corn patch at Eggleston's Springs, where she fell exhausted from hunger
and fatigue on her return from her captivity by the Indians." John New-
ton Harman, Senior, **Harman Genealogy (Southern Branch) with Biograph-
ical Sketches** (W. C. Hill Printing Co., Richmond, Virginia, 1925), p 68.

ferent forms & soops giving her but a little at a time to nurishe her up my mother said although Harmon had even so much fresh venison & Bear meat in the House that he did on the next morning have a fine fat little Beef killed to make Beef soop for her and by Bathing her feet and leggs got her in a day or two that she could travell having severale Horses they got them fixed and one for her to rid brought her on up to the Dunkert Bottom where the fort was and the only one near, and where all the people that were in the country had collected. Thus ended her tryals and defiqualteys of nearly 5 month from the time she was taken prisoner & 42½ days of that time in her returning back in the wilderness when my mother fell in with Harman and his sons related to him the circumstance of leaving the old woman behind & what had transpired and tryed to prevail on him to send his sons in persuit of her but from understanding the treatment which she had received from the old Woman he refused to go[5] However the old woman was more lucky than my mother was alittle above where my mother left her the old woman fell in at a nother place where some Hunters had mad a settlement & built a Cabbin   The Hunters had but just left the place & had left a kettle nearly full of cooked venison & Bear Meat that old woman feasted on it and rested herself for a day or two The Hunters had also left a pair of leather small clothes which she also got drawed on & In additton had left an old horse providence seemed to provide for her the old ladey getting some of what is called Leatherwood bark & making a kind of bridle or halter & caught the old horse & mounted him and persued on her Journey but there is one circumstance

[5] "1755. It is presumed that he and his oldest brother, **Adam**, were the sons who, with their father, the elder Adam Hermann, rescued **Mrs. Ingles** on her return to New River, after her four months' captivity by the Indians."   Ibid, p. 72.

which occurred which may seeme strange at the time they stole the Horse at the nation to bring off their corn the beast had on a bell and when they were obliged to leave the beast in the drift pile the old duch woman took off the bell & brought it the whole trip through all her extremity & distresses, However when my mother got up to the fort she prevailed on some of the men to go in pursuit of the old woman and after traveling 15 or 20 miles down New river met the old woman riding a leg aside on her old horse with the bell on him open & every once in a while wood Hallow that she might be discovered in case any person might be near However the men took her on up to the fort where my mother was and it was certainly a Joyful meeting where they were releaved of all their toyles & defiqualeys, at the time my mother got Back my Father and uncle John Draper had been gone sometime to the Cherokee Nation of Indians with a view to get some of them to go to the Shawneys & to try to purchace their wives & children or to try to procure their releas in some way or other Those two tribes being at peace with each other and thinking this plan might be the most favorable one they could devise, and on the very night after my mother returned to the fort at the Dunkerd Bottom my Father & Uncle Draper lay within a bout 7 miles of the fort on their return & you may guess what was the sensation and feeling of my Father & mother at his arriving at the fort the next day at so unexpected meting (my Aunt Draper did not get released untill about 6 years afterwards, the Circumstances of her Releas is not recolected) However my Father and mother continued at the Dunkert bottom untill the next spring and as the settlers in this country was likely to be Harrassed by the Indians again that season my mother became very restless and uneasy and could not be reconsiled

18

to stay there. My father to gratify her moved her about 20 miles to another fort called Vauses fort on the Head of roanoak where there was more famileys collected & a much stronger fort and more men to gard it but as the Indians was making Depredations on the fronteers she still could not rest reconsiled to stay there my father then moved Her down into Bedford Countey below the blue ridge and in the Cource of that fall there was a strong partey of French & Indians came on to Vauses fort attacked it and finally took the fort & killed and captured all the fameleys that was there and had it not been through the drection of a kind providence that my mother had gone from this fort she wood have fallen into their savage Hand again & wood have been killed or taken prisoner the second time There was some circumstances which I have frequantly heard my father relate as respects two uncles of his and their familey which was at the fort when it was taken (To wit) John & Mathew Ingles The former being out from the fort when it was attacked Hearing the firing of the guns made towards the fort as fast as he could and on coming in sight found the fourt Intirely surrounded by the Indians his famiely being in the fort made an attempt to rush through the Indians to get to his famiely but the Indians discovering him aiming for the fort got around him he still rushed on with his gun in his hand untill they closed in so near that he shot his gun off at them They then closed in on him still beating them off with his gun untill he broke it all to peaces & then with the Barrele untile he got very near to the fort before they overpowered & killed him⁶ The Other brother Mathew was taken prisoner and

⁶"John was killed at Vause's Fort and his wife, Mary, was carried into captivity. When this Mary Ingles returned she married John Miller and went to Carolina." F. B. Kegley, **Kegley's Virginia Frontier** (The Stone Press, Roanoke, Va., U.S.A., 1938), pp. 194-195.

after the indians had started to move off with their plunder & prisoners after getting on some little Distance they all stopped to arrainge some of their fixings. This Mathew Ingles not being confined some of the Indians offended him in some way being a stoubt strong man there happened to be a frying pan lying near where he was he caught hold on the pan & put his foot in the Bowl of the pan & rung off the handle and fell to work on the Indians and knocked them down whenever he could get in reach of them untill they overpowered him and got the pan handle from him This bold darring attempt pleased the Indians so well that they treated him with more respect than any of the other prisoners while ever — he was with them & he got released some years after & returned to the Country again. My father & mother continued to live in Bedford County for severale years in the menetime the settlers was still moving to the Western Watters & extending the settlements to a considerable extent west of New River my father returned to New River with his familey and got himself settled again although the Indians still was harrassing the fronteer every season for many years after his return his familey escaped their depredations although the familys in the neighborhood was obliged almost every season to collect in forts and there was one at his Own Hows when there was a good many collected every year at one time there was a partey of Indians about 8 or 10 passed by new river settlements & being no settlements untile they got belowe the blue ridge on the Head of Smiths River they there killed and Destroye a familey or two & stole severale Horses to bring off their plunder that they had taken and also a woman and 2 or 3 Children prisoners and on their way back had camped within 6 or seven miles of my fathers fort to rest a day at a place where there had been a settlement and a Hows built it so happened that one of the men from the fort went out the day the Indians was there on the Hunt of some of their Horses & happened to discover the Indians he returned amidiately to the fort & gave the alarm there being severale men at the place my father raised 15 or 18 men amediately & persued to attack them though it being too late in the day before the company could start to get where the Indians was to attack them that eavening were detained untile some time in the morning of the next day before my father & the men got to the place where the Indians had camped & the Indians had started from the place However they took their trail and followed as the Indians had not gone more than a half of a mile till they stoped & had kindled a fier and was kookking their Breachfas they not suspecting any danger was Intierly off their gard my fathers partey Crawled up tolerable near & fired on them before they knew anything of them However they flew to their guns and mad every resistance they coud to save themselves & their propertey but being overpowered by the white (M.S. faulty) those that escaped being killed, run off leaving all they had behind them (M.S. faulty) was 6 or 7 Indians killed and they got severale Horses which was packed & the women & Children that was prisoners. There was one of the white men killed. This being the first and onley Defeat which the Indians ever met with in this section of Country and from that time never ventered so fare through the settlement again The Imigration to the West releaved the Settler about New River in a great measure of their Harrassed situation and at length Injoyed peace & prosperity (M.S. marked out; but the fronteer settlements was still Harrassed by the Indians every year for many years after my Father returned to New River with his Familey). My father and mother lived and raised a small familey of 5 children 2 sons & 3 daughters who sustained as respectable Charectors as aney in the whole country my father died in the year 1782 at the age of 53 years my mother still continued to live in New River & Injoyed an extraordinary portion of good health after all her tryals & Defiqualteys untile the year 1815 & dyed at the advanced age of 83 or 84 years of age.

I now return to give a narative of the life and acurrences which Hapened to the two Infant children which was taken captives with my mother shortley after they were separated from my mother at the nation & my mother taken on to the big bone Lick or left the Indians the youngest brother George dyed in the nation the elder brother Thos continued thirteen years & trained up in their savage state that he become intierly accustomed to their Habits & much of an Indian as any of them I can recolect of his telling me of severale Acurrences that Happened him while there & which I think deserves notice One espetially was when he was still small his Indian father and One other Indian as was their ysual Custom to go off some distance from the nation to Hunt & provid meet & his old father taking him on with them after being in the woods some time the Indian father took very sick the other Indian provided some wood and fixed it so that he could make fier for his sick father & gave him directions bringing him watter etc started to the nation 40 or 50 miles to get Help to convey the sick man Home However the verry night after the other Indian left him his old father dyed it also happened that a very deep snowe fell and there he was a lone whithe the dead Indian it also took the other Indian severale days to perform his Journey & return However he had lerned how to keep up his fier and to kook his previsions also at night he wood stele by close up to the dead indians back & cover himself with the blanketts he had & slept very comfortable though it was so long before the other Indian returned that the dead one began to smele the wolves being very plentey they were likeley to attack him and wood come so near that he was freequantley obliged to get up and throw chunk of fier at them to keep them out of the camp The Indians gun was there but he had never

23

attempted to shot a gun However he thought he wood try
and one morning after being very much pestered by the
wolves all the night before got the old indians gun & am-
munition & he had taken some notice of the Indians in the
manner they had loded & put in a smale charge the first
time and there being a good many wild pigeons about the
camp he thought he wood try to shoot some of them & after
severale tryals found he coud kill the pigeons he then concluded he wood be a match for the wolves that night loded
his gun very well but not being strong enough to hold the
gun with out supporting her on something to rest her on
he got the Indians tomehock & Cut a forked stick drove it
in the ground so that he coud rest his gun on it right in a
direction of a path that he had made to the spring & which
path the wolves always came along at night when they wood
come to attact him and amidiately when night came on the
wolves be gan to geather & Howl ale a round his camp he
got his gun & placed it in his forked stick presently the
wolves came Howling along up the path nearly up to his fier
he fiered his gun at them and nocke one down dead The allarm of the gun drove off the others & by that means saved
the dead carcas of the Indian and his own life untile the
other Indians came to his releaf. another circumstance which
happened while he was with them which proved somewhat
Injurous to hisself it was a custom with the Indians to
shoot with a Bow & Arrows One day in trying to shoot
a woodpecker off of a tree it was near where the Indians
had a large fier for the purpose of Barbacuing some meet
in watching the woodpecker & going backward went into
the Hot embers & fier and burnt his feet so much that they
never grew after to their natural size those are the Only
events that I now recolect of hearing him mention

My father had tryed many means to try to recover
him failed in all untile there was a man of the name of
Thos Baker who had been prisoner with the Indians &
had lived in the same nation with my brother Thos Had
by some means got redeemed & came home my father Imployed Baker to go to the nation & purchase my Brother
it being at a time when they were at Peace whith the
Whites Baker undertook the business and went to the Indian town where my Brother lived & made a purchase of
him from his Indian father for something like 100 or 150
dollars & started with him for home having him somewhat
confined for fear of his running a way but Having to pass
by severale Indian villiges on his way hame the squaws got
a chance of talking with the little fellow & persuaded him
to run away from Baker However Baker kep him confined untile he got 40 or 50 miles past ale the Indian viliges
Thinking him intierly safe let him loos and at night when
they lay dow to sleep Baker took little Thos. in his arms
thinking in case he wood attemp to move that he wood
awake but behold when Baker a woke the little fellow had
sliped out of his armes & was gone Baker returned to the
Indian vilege but could not get him the squaws keeping him
conseald was obliged to come off and leave him & return
home However my father stile being antious to get my
brother released from his Heathen State of life a year or
two after Bakers first affort my Father Hiered Baker to
go with him & started the second time with ale nessesarey
preperations for the Journey which was a very disastrous
one in having to go by the way of Winchester thence on by
pitsburg and down on the other side of the Ohio River &
through severale of the indian towns to where my brother
lived being the onley way that could be traveled with any
kind of safety as it was an Intierly a wilderness nearley

from where my father lived to the nation and intierly un-
explored by any white man they persued on to pitsburg but
when ariving there found that the Indians had brok out
in ware against the Whites & was driving all the fronteer
settlers before them and was obliged again to return without accomplishing his purpose & had to wate untile war
subsided my father & Baker again started and went on
my Father thinking it wood be a good article and One that
might add in the inducement in the purchase of his son
from his Indian father though a very impruend One took
severale smale Keggs of rum When getting a mong the
Indians their great thirst for the rum Induced my father
to let them have some not thinking of the Consequances by
their getting drunk They attempted to kill him and would
certainly have affected their purpose had not the squaws
hid him & kept him hid until they got sober However
they persued on through many other defiqualteys untile they
got to the Town my brother lived which was at the mouth
of the Siote when gettin through he found that my brother
had gone with his old Indian father to Detroit and his onley
chance to get him then was to wait there untile they returned his situation was a very dangerous one but fineley
Determined to wait their return by Baker Having severale
acquaintance in the nation having been prisoner with them
before & also my Father Having a verry good natural turn
to please those whome he was among the Indians became
very friendley & very much attached to them and after wat-
ing there about 13 days the old Indian & my brother returned and on my brothers lerning who my father was he
took an attachment to him and was perfectly willing to come
home with him and after paying his old Indian father a
pritey round price for him again started on toward home
the little fellow never showing any Disposition to leave him

& becoming more & more attached to my father tile he got home it is hard for me to express the feelings of a tender mother of Once more receiving to her armes her Affectionat child that had been absent 13 long years from her little Thomas as he might be Justly called so altho 17 years old at that time was very much under the common size of common boys of his age & an entier Indian in his manner & apearance & could not speake one word of English and although he was restored to his friends a relatives his heathen customs & manners was so different to (?) that he became very restless & uneasy and it was with considerable defiqualtey he could be reconciled to stay though my Father & mother both using ale means of reconciling him & Humouring him in their power he wood take pets at times and wood start off and be gone 2 or 3 days at a time which occationed his parents great distress for fear that he wood not return However by Indulging him & Humouring him in all his little fits become more and more reconciled it was with considerable defequalty in getting him to change his Indian custom of wearing his clothes & shooting with his Bows & Arroes & such amusements as he had been accustomed to but by using a good deal of pains to Improve him & to lern him to speak the English language and got him some what sivolized my father sent him down the Country to Abemarl County to old Dr. Walkers to go to school after being there a while he Improved very much in manners & also in learning & became a very good English schollar but never became entierly broke of some of his little Indian actions after remaining there 3 or 4 years returned home quite sivolized, not long after his return home he engaged in the campaign which was going Out against the Indians under Gen'l Charles Lewis who Had the battle with the Indians at point Plesent Mouth of the Great Kanawa Thos. Ingles was in the detachment which was under Col Wm. Christian which was a little in the rear of the main Army and was not present in the time of the inguagement but got up to the place the same night after the action He was One of the troops which was stationed there the winter following and when the treaty of peace was confirmed & the Indians came to the point he fell in with a great many of his old acquaintances & went on home with them to the town & stayed some time with them The season following the troop at the Point was discharged & he returned home Some time after his return he got maryed to a Miss Elliner Griles He then settled on a Creek called Wolf Creek a branch of New River[7] After living there a few years moved to a valuable tract of land his father gave him on the head of the Blue stone, a nother Branch of New River and continued there 1 or 2 years[s] But finding his family was so much exposed to the perpetual depredations of the Indians & being one of the most frunteer settlements and nearley right on a tract where the Indians passed repeatedly to kill & plunder not thinking himself nor familey safe there moved about 15 or 20 miles more to the Heart of the settlement into a place called Burks Gardain it was a situation which there was settlements all around but none within 10 or 12 miles[9] This Burks Gardain is a large tract of land intierly surrounded by a large Mountain and no Other familey living in the place but his own excepting an old Batcheler and his negro boy

[7]"Shortly after his marriage his father gave him a tract of land on Wolf Creek, in the present Giles County." William C. Pendleton, **History of Tazewell County and Southwest Virginia 1748-1920** (W. C. Hill Printing Company, Richmond, Virginia, 1920), p. 444.
[s]"He and his family remained a year or two on Wolf Creek, and then removed to Abb's Valley, where he settled on the one thousand acre tract his father had purchased from the Loyal Company." Pendleton, p. 444.
[9]"He then located with his family in Burke's Garden on the tract of land where James Burke had once lived, and occupied the house Burke had built." Pendleton, p. 444.

of the name of Joseph Hix that lived a bout two miles from
him and his situation might have thought to have been safe
as to the excurtions of the Indians being so localey situated
& settlements all round and more exposed to danger However after living there severale years in the spring of 1782
a partey of Indians found their way into Burks Gardain
and one morning after my brother had gone out into his
plantation where a negroe fellow was at plow my brother
was alarmed by hearing an unusual noise towards the Hows
Ran towards the Hows and when he came in sight saw his
Hows surrounded by a partey of Indians and having no
chance of rending any releaf to his familey returned to
where the fellow was plowing Cut loos the Horses and each
of them Mounting a horse took of for the nearest settlement on the Head of the north fork of Holston in what is
called the Rich Valleys[10] it so hapened that there was a Capt
(?) had called a muster of men on that day He got to
the muster ground a little after the middle of the day
being nearley 20 miles from where he started On giving
the alarm there was 15 or 20 men amediately volunteered
to go in persuit of the Indians However as each man had
to go home or to get his necessary aquipments for his (?)
it was night before they could meet to Persue. There was
12 or 15 men started & it was sometime in the morning of
the next day before they could get to the place[11] when my
brother got back to his place could not find any appearance
of any part of his familey & his Hows burnt up and all in

[10]"Though Ingles had moved to the Garden for safety, in April, 1782,
a large party of Shawnees, led by the noted chief, Black Wolf, entered
Burke's Garden." Pendleton, p. 444.
[11]"It happened to be muster day for Washington County militia and
the settlers on the North Fork of Holston River had assembled, and were
being drilled by Captain Thomas Maxwell, who had formerly lived at the
head of Bluestone, in Tazewell County. Maxwell, with a party of fifteen
or twenty volunteers, went with Thomas Ingles to Burke's Garden to pursue the Indians and rescue the captives." Pendleton, p. 445.

it except what the Indians had taken off   He was then in
hopes that the indians had not killed aney of the familey
and had taken them all as prisoners   The men then agreed
to persue them   The Indians had taken his wife and 3
Children a negroe fellowe & a negroe wench his eldest child
a little daughter about 5 years old called Mary a little son
about 3 years old named William & a little daughter at
the mothers bres 6 or 9 months old   The Indians after
plundering the Howse & taking such things as they needed
or coud carrey off set the Hows on fier and Burnt it up and
then packed the two negroes with what they could carry
and each one taking what he could started off with their
prisoners it so happened that at the very time the Indians
attacked the Hows the old man Wm. Hix & His negroe
who lived about 2 miles off was going to the hows but in
getting in sight of the Hows discovered the indians he amediately took back and both him and the negroe boy ware a
fot the old man ran on However across the mountain another direction from where my brother went to another
settlement and gave the alarm & raised 5 or 6 men & came
on back and got to the place shortley after my brothers
partey got there   They all Joined in the pursuit   They
were all men well trained in following indians trails   The
Indians being some what suspitious that they might be pursued and every precaution on leving no sighn that they
coud prevent and as they were obliged to pass through
some part of the settlement of What is called Clinch Settlement They moved on very causiously & but slowly The
white men got their trail & persued it on to the settlement
of Clinch it so happened that there was at the very time
a campane of Malitia stationed on the frontear as a gard
to the settlers & when my Brother and His partey got to
Clinch there was some more men Joined his partey

& strenghened his partey to a bout 21 men & getting some more supplys in provisions etc persued on after the indians had got clear of the settlement intierly and not being persued as they thought began to be a little more negligent putting out their signs However the persuing partey using all diligance and after 5 or 6 days persuit discovered they were gaining upon the Indians and persuing with much caution & the indians begening to think themselves nearley out of danger became still more tarder & cearless However on the 6 or 7 day that the had been in persuit the spies who kep a hed discovered the indians in the eavening where the Indians had taken up Camp They returned to the partey and gave the information The company concluded that they wood lay back and try to asertain the situation of the ground & incampment that night & not to attact them untile day ligh the next morning They arrainged their plan and a Capt Maxwell who had the command of the company was to crole round in the night with one half of the me to the apposit sid of the camp from where they were & bring on the attact at day light my brother Thos was to crawl up with his partey on the near sid & ly in wait till Maxwell attacked them on the other unfortunately Maxwell in trying to get to his pint got off from the Camp & Coud not find it My Brother & his partey got up within a few feet of the Camp under a bank & was lying waiting every moment for Maxwell to fall on them daylight beginning to break the indians begining to wake up & to move about the men was at lenth discovered[12] The Indians took the allarm & began to tomehock

<hr>

[12] "On the fifth day after the capture the advance scouts of the white men discovered the Indians, who were encamped for the night in a gap of Tug Mountain. A consultation was held by the pursuers, and it was agreed that Captain Maxwell should take half the men, and, during the night, get around to the front of the Indians, and Thomas Ingles should remain with the other half at the rear; and that at daybreak a simultaneous attack upon the savages be made by the two divisions. The night was very dark and the ground exceedingly rough and brushy. Consequently the party with Maxwell lost their way and did not reach the front by daylight." Pendleton, p. 445.

the prisoners my brothers partey Jumped in uppone them
as quick as they possibly coud my brother Jumped into the
Camp and got Hold of his wife While the Indians was trying to tomehock his wife it was a most unlucky surcum-
stance all though my Brother was well aware in their being
discovered that their firs effort wood be to kill the prisoners
& mentioned it to all the men that they might be apprised
although with all the exertions they could use the Indians
accomplished their end   They tomehocked his wife & two
of his children the two elder the one at the breast escaped
& the two negroes his little son was so badly wounded that
he dyed before they left the ground his little Daughter
lived 3 or 4 (M.S. faulty) and then dyed   His wife was
very badly cut in two or three places in her Head but re-
covered after extracting 13 pieces of her scule bone before
it got well   It is astonishing to think althou the men
Jumped into the Camp a mediately they found they ware
Discovered & shot severale guns at them that the indians
all escaped & with most of their arms & another unfortun-
ate circumstance Maxwells party had got a half a mile off at
the time & the Indians on making their escape run right
through Maxwells men & Maxwell Having on a White Hunting shirt one of the Indians shot him through the Boddey
& Killed him it was always thought by the partey that
they had killed some of the Indians but if they did they
got off and so secreetted themselves that they could not be
found   They were obliged to Continue on the ground untill
late in the day on the account of my Brothers little son
dying & Maxwells being killed to try to Bury them in some
manner   While they were detained there they frequantly
Could hear a noise like a person groaning in the agoneys of
death and still serched to find it thinking it to be one of
the Indians who was shot but the Lorrell & Brush being

so thick they could not find him after getting all fixed
they all started back for the nearest settlement of Clinch
which took them about 4 days to purform on account of my
Brothers wife and little daughter being both Badly wounded
and weak about the time the partey got to the Head of
Clinch my father who had gone on there from New River
and luckiley had taken on with him a Doctor met them but
my Brothers little daughters scule being so much fractured
with the tomehock that she dyed the next day after they
returned to the settlement However the Doctor rendered
infinite survice to my brothers wife and after proper application for a few days rendered her able to travell and all
the familey there was left started for New River and in
the cource of a few month my Brothers wife got intirely
well. My Brother continued on New River that season
with his family though at that time the Hoolston Country
was for settling and the Eastern part of Tennessee & my
Brother Thos still inclining to be on the frunteer settlements on account of rainge & raising stock moved to Tenn.
and settle on the Wakaugua a branch of Holston River at
a time that there was but few settlers in that country & a
good deal exposed to the depredations of the Cherokee Indians who frequantly committed Depredations on the
frunteer settlements & killed the settlers he continued there
5 or 6 years untill he got himself tolerable comfortably fixed
so as to live in plenty the people beginning to settle tolerable thick around him he began to get uneasy & restless to
get farthur on to the west where he could have more room,
sold out & moved about 50 miles lower dow the Holston
River and settled on a creek called Mossey Creek then almost an intier fronteer is a country affording a delightfull
summer rainge and plenty of corn for winter range for
stock but laboured under the same defiqualteys as to the

dangerous situation as to his familey exposure to the **depre-**
dations of the Indians though he continued unmolested and
improved Another very good plantation & comfortable fixed
but the settlers still followed him & setling thick all around
him as usual began to get restless & uneasey & about that
time there was a parcele of troops sent down the Holston
River & built a fort at this place where Knoxvill now is
& called fort Knox for the purpose of Having some check
on the Indians in committing depredations on the frontiers
and not long after Fort Knox was erected my Brother Thos
sells out his possessions on Mossey Creek and moves his
familey down to the neighbourhood of fort Knox & settles
again intierly exposed to the depredations of the Indians
and although there were frequant Hostile parteys of Indians passing and committing depredations on the settlements his familey escaped & the country soon became settled
& the town of Knoxvile began to Improve However my
Brother Thos continued on the place which he settled near
Knoxvile & Improved it as usual and got himself Comfort-
abley fixed again & procured severale other Tracts of land
in that neighbourhood and had got his familey pritey well
raised up and one of his daughters marryed & rather seemed
to be settled for the remainder of his life but Hearing of
a man who was owing him a considerable sum of money &
run off being at Natches & understanding that he might
secure the debt in case he went there (M.S. faulty)   His
Head that he wood go and see him at any rate and as it
was a long and teadious rod to travell by land & mostly
through an indian Country though friendley, the Chicasaws,
he concluded rather to run the risque of going by watter
& although there was freequantly Boats running down the
river from Knoxvile to Natcheys & Orleans he concluded
it wood expedite his journey to go in a smale Boat and pro-

34

cured a Bote for the purpose. Ther was 2 or 3 other men
to accompany him on a trading expedition They got ale
ready & started & went on very well untile they came to
the Mustle Shoals in the Tennessee River They attempted
to pass them without a pilot The sholes being more defiqualt
& rougher than they expected and after getting nearley
through their Bote upset & threw the men and all their
(M.S. faulty) into the river & all the chance for their own
escape was by swiming or holding to the Bote as it so happened where they were upset was not fare from the shore
my brother Thos though an exolent swimmer stile Hung
to the Bote & the current stile drifting him near on to the
bank at length he was so near that by the assistance of
some friendley Indians which was in view aiding him got
him and the Bote stoped but what was most remarcable
when the Bote upset my brothers saddle baggs which had
all his clothes & what money he had with him in it some-
how or other in the scuffele caught in one of his armes &
he hele to it & also with the other to the Bote untile they
got to the shore which was everything that was saved
Their situation was truly a destressing one Severale hund-
red miles from home & right in the midst of Indians all
their clothes & provisions (M.S. faulty) & everything lost
or nearly so onley what my brother saved by holding (M.S.
faulty)—and was at a considerable loss to know what to
do but However the Indians were friendley & agreed to
furnish them with provisions & some other things that they
stood in need of & they finalley concluded to pursue on
their Journey mad the nessessary preparations & started
on again & purformed their Journey. My brothers getting
to Natches made some Inquiry for his man that he went
and at length found him but intierly unable to pay him.
That his Jorney at the risque of his life was ale for noth-

ing thought my brother after viewing this country he became so pleased with it that he wood move his familey to it and on his returning home amediately Sold off all his property at a considerable sacrifice to get to a nother new country as he had formerly done and moved his familey & settled near Natcheys

This last narative was related to me by my Brother himself on his return from that countrey & before he moved his familey after his moving to that countrey I have little or no knowlage what traspired only from Hearsay

1982 NOTES

Location of Draper's Meadows

The present location of Draper's Meadows is on the campus of Virginia Polytechnic and State University at Blacksburg, Virginia. "The Draper's Meadows Massacre July 8, 1755" is inscribed on a small bridge directly across from the Pro Shop of the campus golf course. Another marker, erected by the Allegheny Chapter, D.A.R., Blacksburg, Va., can be seen by the campus road to Smithfield, the Preston's ancestral home. David E. Johnson in his **History of the Middle New River Settlements and Contiguous Territory** wrote, "The Ingles-Draper settlement was called "Draper's Meadow's," but we are told that the name was changed by Colonel William Preston to "Smithfield," in honor of his wife, who was a Miss Smith of Louisa County, Virginia."[13]

"Old Dutch Woman"

The editors would like to point out that the hardships of the journey home were shared equally by the "Old Dutch Woman" and acknowledge her efforts and courage.

Accurate Measurement of Part of the Route Home

Mr. Cecil C. Lawson, certified land surveyor, using U.S. Geological survey maps found the total distance of the river route from Bigbone, Kentucky, to Eggleston, Virginia, to be 449 miles. No one knows how many miles were added to this total by the detours which Mary Draper Ingles and her companion, the "Old Dutch Woman" were forced to take.

Since the three rivers, the New, the Kanawha, and the Ohio all flow toward the Mississippi, Mary Draper Ingles and her companion were traveling upstream and so could not utilize the currents of these streams to speed their return home.

---

13. Johnson, David E. **A History of Middle New River Settlements and Contiguous Territory.** Huntington, West Virginia: Standard P.T.G. and Pub. Co., 1906, p. 9.

Subject: River Route From Bigbone, Ky To Eggleston, Va.
Total Distance of 449 Miles

MILES		LOCATION
0.0		Bigbone, Ky.
2		Ohio River
10		Rabbit Hash
20		Aurora
44		Ludlow
52		Fort Thomas
65		New Richmond
87		Augusta
88		Edge Map
97		Ripley
105		Maysville
117		Manchester
130		Rome
140		Buena Vista
156.5		Scioto River
158		Portsmouth
162		New Boston
166		Wheelersburg
186		Russell
189		Coal Grove
191		Ashland
197		Kenova
203		Huntington
219		Green Bottom
242		Gallipolis
245.5		Kanawha River
254.5		Edge of Map
260		Arbuckle
281		Plymouth
292		St. Albans
303		Charleston
322		Cedar Grove
334		Alloy
340		Gauley Bridge
346.5		Hawks Nest
357		Edge Map

Ohio River 245.5 Miles

Kanawha River 94.5 Miles

New River

MILES		LOCATION
374		Terry
377		Laurel Creek
386		Meadow Creek
398		Hinton
399.5		Greenbrier River
428		Rich Creek
432		Narrows
444		Pembroke
449		Eggleston, Va.

New River 109 Miles

Note: - This data is from maps of U.S. Geological Survey.
Scale: 1:250,000

U.S. Geological Survey - Reference Maps
Louisville NJ 16-6 - 1956
Cincinnati N.J 16-3 - 1964
Huntington NJ 17-4 - 1966
Charleston NJ 17-5 - 1966
Bluefield NJ 17-8 - 1967

COMMONWEALTH OF VIRGINIA
CECIL C. LAWSON
CERTIFICATE NO.
709
CERTIFIED LAND SURVEYOR

Cecil C. Lawson, C.L.S.
Oct. 12, 1970